The Kids' Career Library™

A Day in the Life of a
Newspaper
Reporter

Mary Bowman-Kruhm and Claudine G. Wirths

The Rosen Publishing Group's
PowerKids Pre

New York

Published in 1999 by The Rosen Publishing Group, Inc.
29 East 21st Street, New York, NY 10010

Copyright © 1999 by The Rosen Publishing Group, Inc.

First Edition

Book Design: Erin McKenna

Photo Illustrations: All photo illustrations by Ethan Zindler.

Bowman-Kruhm, Mary.
    A day in the life of a newspaper reporter / by Mary Bowman-Kruhm and Claudine G. Wirths.
        p.   cm. — (The kids' career library)
    Includes index.
    Summary: Describes the job of a newspaper reporter by following his daily activities as he meets with his editor, attends a press conference, does research, and writes his story.
    ISBN 0-8239-5306-8 (alk. paper)
    1. Fulwood, Sam. 2. Journalists—United States—Biography—Juvenile literature. 3. Reporters and reporting—United States—Juvenile literature. [1. Journalists. 2. Occupations.]
    I. Wirths, Claudine G. II. Title. III. Series.
PN4874.F775B69 1998
070'.92—dc21
                                                                                    98-17483
                                                                                       CIP
                                                                                       AC

Manufactured in the United States of America

Contents

A Reporter's Job

Sam Fulwood is a newspaper reporter. Like all reporters, his job is to find out the *who, what, where, when, why,* and *how* of every story. Then he must write the story.

Reporter Fulwood writes for a newspaper in California called the *Los Angeles Times*. But he works in a tall building in Washington, DC. From Washington, he tells his readers what happens in the capital city of the United States.

◀ Reporter Fulwood works in Washington, DC, the nation's capital. Important news happens there every day.

Who and When?

When Reporter Fulwood arrives at work, he meets with his **editor** (EH-dih-ter).

"What story are you going to work on?" the editor asks.

Reporter Fulwood and the editor decide he will cover a **press conference** (PRES KON-frents). The *who* in his story will be the person who talks at the press conference. The *what* will be the event that will be discussed at the press conference. They also talk about what **angle** (ANG-ul), or point, the story will have.

Reporter Fulwood's editor gives him advice and help when it's needed. ▶

What, Where, Why, and How?

At the press conference, Reporter Fulwood hears about a new plan for schools. He also finds out *where* and *how* the plan will be carried out and *why* this plan will help schoolchildren in the United States.

"I know the *who, what, where, when, why,* and *how,*" Reporter Fulwood thinks as he leaves the press conference. "But I still have to find out more."

◀ Reporter Fulwood listens very carefully at press conferences so he gets all the facts.

Finding More Facts

Reporter Fulwood talks to other people about the new plan. He asks them many questions. Some people like the plan for schoolchildren. Others don't think the plan will work. Fulwood wants to hear many different points of view.

Reporter Fulwood works hard to get the full story. He is proud of the work that he does. He studied hard to become a reporter and wants to do the best work that he can.

Fulwood asks many people about the plan for schoolchildren. He wants as much ▶ information as he can find.

Work Tools

Reporter Fulwood returns to his office to do more work on the story. His telephone and his computer help him. These are his tools.

Reporter Fulwood is on the phone for much of the day. He talks to many people to check his facts again and again. He also uses his computer for **research** (REE-serch), or finding out more facts. He types notes for his story. He also e-mails letters from his computer.

◀ Sometimes Reporter Fulwood will sit at his desk all day when he works on a story.

A New Angle

As he works, Reporter Fulwood has a new idea. He tells the editor about a different angle he wants to use on the story. With his new angle, the story would be written from Fulwood's point of view.

"My story will take about twenty inches," Fulwood tells the editor. Twenty inches of a newspaper story is about as many words as there are in this book. Newspaper stories are measured in inches because there is only a certain amount of space for each story in the newspaper.

"Great idea. Go ahead," his editor says.

The editor will work with Reporter Fulwood to make the angle of his story more clear. ▶

Hurry!

At 3:00, Reporter Fulwood sits down to write his story. He must write quickly to meet his **deadline** (DED-lyn). But he can't write too fast! He knows a good reporter must tell a story in a way that people will understand it. Suddenly, the phone rings.

"I have some facts you can use for your story," the person says.

The phone rings again and again. People also stop to talk to him. Reporter Fulwood has learned to keep writing even with all of these **interruptions** (in-tuh-RUP-shunz).

◀ Sometimes Fulwood has to do two or three things at once. He's a busy man!

Into Print

By 5:00 Reporter Fulwood has finished the story. The *who, what, where, when, why,* and *how* are there. But he has written the story from a special point of view. That is what makes Reporter Fulwood a good reporter.

Reporter Fulwood and his editor check the story again. The editor always has the final word on what is printed in the paper.

Then the story is sent by computer to the newspaper's home office in California. Soon the story will be printed and ready to read.

Fulwood may ask for other reporters' opinions on his story before it's printed. ▶

Many Days Are Different

    Every day is unique. Sometimes Reporter Fulwood will spend a whole day in meetings. Another day he may appear on a TV show. He may write all day. He may travel anywhere a story is happening to speak with people who want to answer his questions—and even to people who don't!

    Most of the time reporters work on their own. Being a reporter is a good job for a person like Sam Fulwood. He likes to be **independent** (in-dee-PEN-dent).

◀ Reporter Fulwood is always ready to cover a story, no matter where it is.

A Busy Life and a Busy Mind

No matter what he does, Reporter Fulwood juggles three stories in his mind: the one he is writing today, the one he wrote yesterday, and the one he will write tomorrow.

He must meet the deadline for today's story. He must write about anything new that happened since yesterday's story was printed. And he must plan tomorrow's story and the angle he'll use on it.

Reporter Fulwood has a busy life. He enjoys his career as a reporter.

Glossary

angle (ANG-ul) The special point of a story; the special way a story is written.

deadline (DED-lyn) When a project must be finished.

editor (EH-dih-ter) The person in charge of giving the final okay for stories written by reporters.

independent (in-dee-PEN-dent) Thinking for or taking care of oneself.

interruption (in-tuh-RUP-shun) A stop in the middle of what someone is doing.

press conference (PRES KON-frents) A planned meeting in which someone introduces an idea to reporters and they ask questions.

research (REE-serch) To carefully study something to find out more about it.

23

Index

24